Original title:
Pine and Poetry

Copyright © 2025 Creative Arts Management OÜ
All rights reserved.

Author: William Hawthorne
ISBN HARDBACK: 978-1-80567-280-7
ISBN PAPERBACK: 978-1-80567-579-2

Whispers in the Evergreen

In the woods where squirrels reside,
They chatter loudly; they cannot hide.
A tree puts on its best green dress,
While birds debate who's more of a mess.

The roots play tricks beneath the ground,
They tickle toes of those around.
A raccoon writes a tale so tall,
'The forest is the best of all!'

When leaves fall down like confetti,
The trees shake limbs, they're trying to be ready.
A breeze laughs as it twirls about,
Spreading laughter, no room for doubt!

Cadence in the Canopy

In the shade where squirrels dance,
Birds throw a wild, feathery glance.
The branches jiggle, leaves giggle loud,
Nature's party, a chaotic crowd.

A raccoon in a top hat, very sleek,
Juggles acorns, a forest mystique.
With pinecones rolling, the laughter flows,
As the sun dips low, and the wind blows.

Stitched by Spruce

A needle made of twigs does sew,
Winds whisper secrets that only trees know.
With every stitch, a ticklish laugh,
Spruce threads tales in nature's craft.

The owls are giggling, the shadows sway,
As raccoons come out for a nightly play.
Stitched together, each story we find,
In the laughter of leaves, we're all intertwined.

Lines from the Leafy Realm

In a leafy nook, where shadows tease,
A chorus of crickets hums with ease.
Chattering squirrels wear tiny crowns,
While laugh lines grow in the bark of brown.

A curious badger, with spectacles on,
Reads novels in the dusk till the dawn.
With every page, the chuckles rise,
In this green theater under the skies.

Forest Fables and Rhyme

In the heart where the wild things blink,
Mice hold court while the owls think.
Tales of jesters and knights with fur,
The forest chuckles, a joyful stir.

A skunk in a tutu twirls with flair,
While rabbits run races without a care.
With each funny twist, we all align,
In fables of green, where laughter's divine.

A Journey Through the Whispering Woods

In a forest where shadows play,
Trees wear hats, oh what a sight!
Squirrels dance in bright ballet,
Chasing dreams from day to night.

A rabbit reads a tale out loud,
While owls hoot in soft delight.
The acorns gather quite a crowd,
As mischief sparks beneath the light.

The brook hums tunes of silly rhymes,
While frogs jump high with glee and cheer.
Let's all join in for silly times,
Among the whispers that we hear.

So take a stroll, just be careful,
Lest you trip on a dancing root.
In this wood, the sound is powerful,
As laughter sprouts from every shoot.

The Serenity of the Sylvan Bard

A bard with feathers sings a song,
His notes will tickle every ear.
With every word, he can't go wrong,
Even if he sings from fear.

The trees join in a playful jest,
With branches swaying, oh so grand.
The critters laugh and take a rest,
As winds spin tales across the land.

A butterfly flutters in a swirl,
Critics say she's got no style.
Yet up she goes, a fancied twirl,
Proving laughter makes us smile.

So grab your friends, don't be shy,
In this land where joy takes flight.
Let worries drift and spirits fly,
In a world that feels so right.

The Gentle Touch of Nature's Hand

In the forest where squirrels dance,
Giggles echo as branches prance.
A wanderer stumbles, then takes a fall,
Nature laughs, no mercy at all.

Sunlight dapples on leafy hats,
Birds gossip over acorn chats.
With each twist and turn, nature's tease,
Who knew a tree could bring you to your knees?

Secrets Cradled by the Foliage

Whispers travel through the green,
A raccoon plotting, plotting unseen.
Leaves hide secrets, oh what a show,
As nature chuckles, 'Come see the show!'

Beneath the limbs, there's mischief afoot,
A tree frog jumps, making us hoot.
What wonders in greenery unfold,
With tales of the woodlands quietly told.

Harmonies of Hope in the Branches

The wind strums softly on a twig guitar,
Nature's band, we're never too far.
A chorus of crickets, frogs serenade,
In this leafy realm, worries start to fade.

With each breeze, laughter soars high,
And even the clouds seem to sigh.
Beneath the canopy's cheerful grin,
Life plays its tune, let the fun begin!

A Canvas of Canopy Dreams

Twinkling lights greet the night,
Fireflies join the dance, what a sight!
Nature's canvas, painted bright,
Where laughter glimmers, pure delight.

But watch your step, there's a branch!
Or you might find yourself in a clench.
Nature's art is fun, but beware,
Some surprises may leave you in despair!

Stanzas of the Silent Grove

In the woods where silence reigns,
A squirrel dances, pulling chains.
A toad croaks out a quirky beat,
While ants march on with tiny feet.

The trees whisper secrets, oh so sly,
A jay bird mimics, oh my, oh my!
Their laughs are carried on the breeze,
As mushrooms giggle 'neath their leaves.

Echoes of the Tall Trees

Whispers float from branch to branch,
As raccoons throw a wild dance.
A woodpecker joins in with a tap,
While squirrels argue over a map.

The owls hoot with hilarious flair,
They're masters of a midnight dare.
In the tall trees where giggles soar,
Nature's jesters, begging for more.

Ink Beneath the Boughs

In a shady nook with leaves so thick,
A fox tells tales, both sly and quick.
With acorns scattered all around,
Each joke travels swiftly through the ground.

A hedgehog pens a wobbly rhyme,
While critters gather, munching thyme.
Beneath the boughs, laughter untold,
Ink spills stories, funny and bold.

Rhymes in the Canopy

Up in the treetops, laughter flies,
With chirps and caws that twist and rise.
A parrot tells a pun so lame,
While chattering monkeys join the game.

With vines that swing like jovial swings,
The breeze carries the joy it brings.
Giggles echo through leafy halls,
As nature plays its funny calls.

Inked in Needles

Needles prick, a tale unfolds,
With ink from sap, the story's told.
A squirrel laughs at all our woes,
As branches sway, the mischief grows.

Pinecone dresses, quite the sight,
Dancing shadows, day and night.
With every breeze, a chuckle flies,
In this green world, we jest and sigh.

Ode to the Woodland Whisper

In the forest, whispers shriek,
'Why do humans talk so bleak?'
A leaf nods, a grin so wide,
As critters gather, side by side.

With acorns tossed like tiny bombs,
They disguise their pranks as charming psalms.
In every rustle, laughter swells,
Among the trunks, we weave our spells.

A Tapestry of Green

Look at me, clad in all green,
A leafy suit, quite the fashion scene.
With every gust, my branches sway,
Giggling softly, come what may.

The sun shines down, a spotlight bright,
On the woodland stage, oh what a sight!
We dance and prance as critters gawk,
With every rustling, we just mock.

Secrets Woven in Bark

Bark so rugged, secrets lace,
In the wood, there's a funny face.
Knots and curves tell tales of yore,
Of turtles racing and birds that soar.

The moss giggles, 'I'm soft indeed!'
While ants parade, as if on steed.
A riddle here, a pun over there,
In every groove, fun's everywhere.

Inked in Swaying Branches

The wind whispers secrets, oh so grand,
As branches dance, a joke so planned.
Squirrels giggle, chasing with glee,
While I scratch my head, what could it be?

Rustling leaves chuckle, the sky turns bright,
A feathered bard takes off in flight.
My pen in hand, I scribble away,
As laughter echoes through the bright day.

Verses in Verdant Silence

In the shade, where shadows tease,
I sip my drink, a light summer breeze.
The grass seems to whisper, 'What's the score?'
My notebook giggles, begging for more.

A tree takes a bow, leaves in a twist,
An acorn drops, oh, what a missed!
I laugh as I write, thoughts in a swirl,
The forest smiles back, in its leafy whirl.

Evergreen Echoes

The zany woodpecker drums a tune,
While mushrooms wiggle, beneath the moon.
A rabbit hops, with a bow and a grin,
While raccoons plot mischief, hoping to win.

A breeze tickles branches, what fun to behold,
As stories unfold, like tales once told.
I jot down the antics, in a fit of delight,
The woods is a stage, chaos feels right.

Chronicles of the Woods

A lizard sunbathes with an imperial flair,
As ladybugs waddle, without a care.
The wise old owl, with spectacles perched,
Tells tales of the nights when mischief lurched.

Crickets compose, as moonlight fades,
Beneath green giants, the fun never evades.
With a wink and a chuckle, I dance through the glade,
In this wild, whimsical, leafy charade.

Nature's Embrace in Verse

In a forest where squirrels mock,
Trees dance gently, a ticking clock.
Frogs recite their ribbit song,
While owls giggle, "What's wrong?"

Mice in hats play hide and seek,
Chasing shadows, quite unique.
Breezes tell silly jokes galore,
And hummingbirds sing, "More, more!"

Leaves twirl down like dizzy friends,
On their laughter, the day depends.
Underneath the canopy wide,
Nature's jesters play with pride.

With every rustle, a cry of glee,
Echoes tumble from tree to tree.
Here in the green, where spirits roam,
Laughter mingles, we feel at home.

Ghosts of the Ancient Pines

Whispers from the treetops high,
Old trees chuckle, oh my, oh my!
Barking dogs in moonlit dreams,
Keebler elves plan wild, crazy schemes.

Ghostly figures do the dance,
With a twirl and spasmodic prance.
Mossy crowns on heads of ghouls,
Teaching roots to break the rules.

Creaky branches share a tale,
Of how their leaves once set sail.
Winding 'round in twilight's glow,
The ancient shake and still don't know.

But who needs fright on this fine night?
All's a jest, and the mood feels right.
Chortles weave amongst the boughs,
Eternal fun, but few know how.

Whirling Leaves of Imagination

Leaves a'whirl in a merry race,
Twirling with joy, they find their place.
Imagine them dressed in silly gear,
With giggles echoing, loud and clear.

One leaf's a pirate, eye patch and hook,
Another's a wizard from a storybook.
They chat and laugh in vibrant hues,
Sharing secrets of the forest views.

Spinning round like a carnival ride,
Their frolicsome fun can't be denied.
With every gust, they take the flight,
In a comical chase, what a sight!

So join their dance, let worries ease,
In this whimsical world, do as you please.
For when imagination takes to air,
Laughter abounds, free as a hare.

Starlit Soliloquy of the Grove

Under the stars, the night is bright,
Crickets chirp with all their might.
Owls debate the silliest things,
While fireflies don their glowing blings.

In the glen, there's laughter loud,
Echoing through the very proud.
Barkley the raccoon spins a yarn,
While toads clamor for more to adorn.

"Who's the star?" one leaf would croon,
"To be or not, beneath the moon?"
This nightly show, a true delight,
With every chuckle, futures ignite.

So gather 'round, all woodland folk,
Join this dance, share in the joke.
In the grove, where giggles thrive,
Each moment sparkles, fully alive.

Canopy Chronicles

Up in the branches, a squirrel plays,
Chasing his shadow through sunlit rays.
A poet declares, 'Oh, what a sight!'
The squirrel drops nuts, oh what a plight!

With laughter, they tumble, a comical show,
The words from the trees start to flow.
"Why did the acorn refuse to fight?"
"Because it was stumped and lost in plight!"

Evergreen Echoes

In a forest of needles, their whispers tease,
A branch drops a line with a light, breezy ease.
"Why is the tree so tall and grand?"
"Because it knows how to take a stand!"

With laughter among the leaves so green,
They share jokes that are quirky and mean.
"Leaf me alone!" one shouts with glee,
The trees shake their boughs, oh what a spree!

Letters in the Roots

Deep underground, the roots weave tales,
Of gossiping moles and shifty snails.
A worm wiggled by with a curious grin,
"Did you hear the one about the nut that could spin?"

The stories spread, like bark in the breeze,
Giggles erupt, from branches to knees.
"Let's write a letter, make it a trunk!"
"Dear Estelle, your bark has gone bunk!"

Arboreal Anthems

Singing a tune with each gentle sway,
The branches dance in a funny ballet.
The birdies chirp jokes, oh how they sing,
"Why don't trees ever use bling?"

"Because they can't handle the weight of a ring!"
They twirl and they twist, enjoying the zing.
"Let's make a concert, an arboreal spree!"
Under the moon, join the canopy glee!

Nature's Verses Unfurled

In a forest where squirrels conspire,
They rhyme with the wind and never tire.
One yelled out, "Hey! Do you hear this beat?"
While a bird chirped, 'Tis almost a feat!"

Fungi high-five on a log in their pride,
Mushroom hats tip as they sidle and glide.
A rabbit rapped verses, his carrot in tow,
While fireflies twinkled a starlit show.

Among the Pines and Dreams

A tree with a hat, oh what a sight!
He swayed to the rhythm in sheer delight.
Raccoons in tuxedos threw a grand ball,
While owls gave speeches, but none could recall!

A squirrel juggled acorns, a real show-off,
Fell on his tail, and we couldn't scoff.
The breeze joined in with a giggle and laugh,
As branches shook hands with the world's silly half.

Gossamer Breaths of Cedar

With a breeze blowing whispers, oh what a tease,
    Cedar trees chuckle, swaying with ease.
    A spider spun tales, intricate and bright,
While crickets composed tunes under moonlight.

    A ladybug slipped on the tree's smooth face,
    Claimed it was all for a new kind of grace.
    "I'll write about life!" she declared with glee,
But slipped off her perch, 'twas quite a wild spree!

Stanzas Lost in the Woods

In the heart of the thicket, a verse fell askew,
A bear started rhyming, who knew he could do?
With a twist and a shake, he proclaimed his great flow,
As rabbits critiqued, but they didn't quite know!

The plants wrote a manifesto, roots inked in mud,
Accused the sun's rays of being a dud.
As shadows laughed softly, an audience bold,
They cheered for the poems as the night turned to gold.

Nature's Ink in the Underbrush

In shadows deep where critters peek,
A squirrel's stash is quite unique.
With acorns piled like mountain peaks,
He pens his thoughts with tiny squeaks.

The beetle dons a writer's hat,
His story starts with a silly spat.
He claims the leaves are all too flat,
Yet dreams of tales where he is fat.

The mushrooms nod in secret glee,
As tales of mischief swirl the tree.
With ink of sap and roots set free,
They laugh in whispers, can you see?

So wander forth through brush and grove,
Where laughter blooms and stories strove.
Embrace the quirks of nature's trove,
And find the joy in tales we've wove.

The Essence of Endless Green

In grassy fields, the jokes unite,
The daisies giggle, oh what a sight!
The clover sings, with all its might,
"Join in our fun, it feels so right!"

The shade of trees plays hide-and-seek,
While breezes tease, they poke and tweak.
An owl winks, "I'm far from weak,
I hoard the best jokes every week!"

From leaves that rustle, jokes take flight,
As toads recite in pure delight.
A turtle's grin is quite the sight,
He chuckles slow, but laughs just right!

So stop and smell the green so bright,
Embrace the whimsy, hold it tight.
In nature's realm, we find our light,
A world where laughter takes its height.

Verses at Twilight's Edge

As daylight fades, the whispers flow,
The fireflies dance, their strobe light show.
A cricket chirps, "You think you know?
I'm the real star, don't say it slow!"

A hedgehog rolls with a giggling spree,
He spins and twirls, as wild as can be.
"Don't mind me, I'm just fancy-free,
The night's my stage, come watch with glee!"

The moonbeams join this playful frolic,
While flowers blush, feeling symbolic.
"Who needs the sun? We're purely iconic!
With roots in laughter, it's never ironic!"

When stars pop out, the tales take flight,
In nature's theatre, all feels right.
Each verse a giggle, pure delight,
Under the moon, we shine so bright.

Rhymes that Dance on the Breeze

Amidst the sways of playful air,
The whispers shout, "It's only fair!
That dandelions float with flair,
In rhymes and giggles, now beware!"

Bumblebees buzz with silly tales,
Of honeyed dreams and tiny sails.
With pollen grains like painted nails,
They revel in their flowery trails!

A wandering breeze, with a giggly grin,
Turns every twig into a violin.
The nature folk play, where to begin?
In laughter and rhyme, we all win!

So let the laughter float on high,
As butterflies flap, twirling shy.
In every rhyme, we dance and fly,
In this merry world, just you and I!

Forest Floor Elegies

Among the leaves, I trip and fall,
To greet a squirrel, who's quite tall.
He steals my lunch with a cheeky grin,
While I just wonder where to begin.

Mushrooms dance like they're on stage,
In this wild world, I'm quite the sage.
A toadstool laughs as I pass by,
Oh, how they mock—oh, how they sigh!

Ants march proudly, their tiny parade,
While I contemplate the mistakes I've made.
A picnic planned, but I forgot the bread,
Now I'm just here, in this leafy spread.

So here's to earth, in its messy joy,
With worms as friends, and mud to enjoy!
I'll laugh along with the roots below,
As nature puts on a comical show.

Lyrical Greenery

The bushes chat with vibrant cheer,
While I munch snacks without a fear.
The daisies gossip in low tones,
I swear I heard them mention bones!

A tall oak tries a dance of flair,
But ends up tangled, in quite a snare.
His bark's a mess, and leaves go flying,
While nearby, a raccoon keeps on spying.

Laughter echoes in between the ferns,
With trees that take turns in amusing turns.
A cat in the grass poses like a king,
While the flowers bloom, and the bugs take wing.

I sit and chuckle at this grand show,
With a squirrel that's almost ready to blow!
In this verdant hall, where joys combine,
Life's little antics are simply divine.

The Language of Needles

The needles whisper secrets at night,
While the stars above shine super bright.
I ponder what they mean by their sighs,
Could they be sharing my favorite fries?

A hedgehog strolls, in spikey attire,
While nightingales sing with such desire.
But oh, how the crickets like to rave,
Making the night a bit more brave.

Branches sway like they're in a jest,
Trying to out-fun the bees at their nest.
The pines roll their eyes, then join in the jest,
A pine cone falls—oh, what a test!

With laughter swirling among the trees,
Their witty remarks carried by the breeze.
I join their joke, and with them I blend,
In this woodland of laughter, where fun has no end.

Treespeak: A Sonnet

When trees begin to gossip in the shade,
Their branches intertwined in friendly jest.
The wind, a messenger, is not dismayed,
As leaves of humor are their very best.

A woodpecker raps a tune so spry,
While squirrels chuckle at their acorn stash.
With shadows dancing under the wide sky,
I'm just a witness to this lively clash.

In every rustle, every whispered sound,
I find a joke well hidden in the bark.
Each moment precious, hilarity found,
As woodland friends light up the dark.

So join the fun, let laughter grow free,
In this lively place, come laugh with me!

The Scent of Solitude

In the woods where whispers hide,
A squirrel thinks he's taking a ride.
With acorns stacked high on his head,
He dreams of a throne made of bread.

Fragrant breezes tickle his tail,
As he plans out his next little trail.
A dance with shadows, oh so spry,
While a bird just giggles up in the sky.

Leaves giggling down from the bough,
They seem to shout, 'You should take a bow!'
With every step, a soft surprise,
A comedy act that never dies.

In solitude, amidst the trees,
Lies the humor of nature's tease.
So tip your hat to the woodland crew,
For laughter grows where the wild things grew.

Statuesque Sentinels

Standing tall, with arms out wide,
They wear a gown of green with pride.
Their laughter echoes in the breeze,
As squirrels a-hip, they tease with ease.

With knots and twists, they strike a pose,
Like grumpy guardians untouched by woes.
They huff and puff when the wind gets bold,
Still, they listen well to stories told.

While critters scurry without a care,
These silent watchers, stoic, stare.
They plot the next big woodland ball,
And chuckle softly when creatures fall.

With whims and quirks, they sway along,
In a forest where even trees belong.
Statuesque, they'll never break,
Unless a bird takes off with a big old cake.

Leaves that Speak in Rhyme

Whispering secrets in every breeze,
Leaves sing out, making nature's tease.
With acorn hats, the critters chime,
Joining the chorus, they all feel sublime.

A rustling sound, what could it be?
The branches giggle, 'Just wait and see!'
With every flutter, a joke's confined,
In the melody of the forest, entwined.

They share their tales with the light of day,
While shadows dance in a playful ballet.
The breeze brings laughter, a gentle nudge,
In the greenness of the woods, they won't judge.

In fellowship with earthy cheer,
Nature's humor is always near.
Leaves that gossip, so light and free,
Might just send you home with a chuckle or three.

Sylvan Serenade

In twilight's glow, the forest groans,
As creatures gather, they toss their loans.
A hare with a monocle looks so grand,
While the frogs prepare to start a band.

With toads on drums and owls in ties,
They croak and hoot beneath starry skies.
A raccoon strums on a guitar so fine,
Imagining fame, maybe a headline.

The trees sway gently, tapping their feet,
To the rhythm of critters in this grand suite.
Laughter and songs fill the chilly air,
A sylvan serenade beyond compare.

So join the fun in the woodland fest,
Where every creature is truly blessed.
For in this grove, with spirits high,
Even the mushrooms giggle and sigh.

Wistful Writings of the Woods

In the woods where squirrels chat,
They draft their tales on acorn hats.
With plumes of moss, they jot a rhyme,
In laughter's shade, they waste no time.

The owl hoots jokes, a wise old sage,
His punchlines hang like leaves on page.
Rabbits giggle, hop with glee,
As nature's jesters, wild and free.

A hedgehog pens his daily thoughts,
In bramble bushes, he's not distraught.
A cactus joins, all prickly and proud,
Recording punchlines, laughing loud.

Beneath the branches, whispers flow,
As shadows dance, the humor grows.
In these woods, the words take flight,
A merry place, both day and night.

A Symphony of the Silent Trees

In a clear voice, the maples shout,
While cedar chimes with a snoozy clout.
The birches sway with snickers and sway,
Creating tunes to brighten the day.

Firs, they hum like ballad kings,
While dreaming of squirrels and other things.
Their branches wave in comedic flair,
Jokes rustle softly through the air.

The woodpecker's drum provides the beat,
As critters groove on tiny feet.
Each tree a note in spirited song,
With laughter echoing all day long.

A chorus of bark, the root's delight,
Whispering puns till the fall of night.
Nature's jesters, still and free,
Provideres of joy, oh can't you see?

Cradle of the Canopy

Up in the heights where eagles play,
Mischief brews at the end of the day.
Twigs and branches become the bed,
For dreamers with laughter in their head.

The foliage tickles the clouds above,
As squirrels tumble, full of love.
Their acrobatics bring smiles and cheer,
In the cradle where fun keeps near.

The sun peeks through with a playful wink,
Nature's mischief is always in sync.
In this green realm, the giggles collide,
A friendly band with laughter as guide.

And as the stars begin to peek,
The trees share secrets and joy they seek.
A world of chuckles wrapped in green,
Where whimsy reigns, like a playful dream.

Verse Among the Spruces

With spruces tall, they start to rhyme,
In whispered winds, a comical chime.
They sway and bow with a giggling tone,
A dance of humor where seeds are sewn.

The critters gather, take a seat,
On furry cushions, soft and neat.
Raccoons tell tales of the night's charade,
While shadows laugh at the pranks they've played.

As berries blush from nature's jest,
Each line a reflection of woodland zest.
Chirping birds join the frolic and play,
In every corner, laughter holds sway.

So if you stroll through this forest grand,
Hear the chuckles, the joy at hand.
In every corner a witty muse,

The Treetop's Tale

In the canopy high, squirrels dance,
Chasing each other, without a chance.
A chorus of laughter in the tall trees,
Nature's own stand-up, with jokes in the breeze.

Acorns fall down, a hearty thud,
A nutty affair, it's all in good fun.
The wise old owl gives a wink and a grin,
Saying, "In this tree, let the games begin!"

Raccoons hide snacks, a daring heist,
While chipmunks giggle, living their best life.
A trunk full of secrets, no one can see,
In the realm of branches, they all live free.

So next time you wander beneath their height,
Listen for laughter, under the moonlight.
For the trees hold stories, they twirl and twist,
With a wink and a nod, you can't help but miss.

Rhythms of the Bough

Swinging on branches, the songbirds croon,
A cheeky little tune, beneath the moon.
Where the wind plays tricks and leaves swirl around,
Every rustling whisper, is joy to be found.

The branches sway low, to a beat from the sky,
A funky old rhythm, as the clouds drift by.
With every soft creak, a new dance is born,
In the waltz of the woods, every critter is sworn.

A squirrel in shades does a solo spree,
While fragile fawns giggle, just wait and see.
The forest erupts in a burst of delight,
For they are the stars, in the moon's silver light.

So join in the fun, let your spirit be free,
In the garden of giggles, wild and carefree.
For the rhythms of boughs sing a tune so sweet,
And life in a tree is a jolly old treat.

Forest Dreams

Underneath a blanket, soft and green,
A feast of odd dreams, like you've never seen.
A hedgehog in bowties, singing a song,
While rabbits wear slippers, and they dance along.

Beneath the tall trunks, where shadows play,
The forest is loaded with a whimsical way.
Mice in top hats, playing cards for fun,
The laughter of owls, a noisy run.

Where dandelions bloom, and frogs wear crowns,
Each beetle's a general, leading their towns.
A joke in the brambles, a riddle so bright,
In this dreamscape of laughter, it feels just right.

So come take a stroll, in this whimsical place,
Where every soft whisper brings joy to your face.
For the trees hold a magic, quirky and free,
In these forest dreams, you're just meant to be.

Written in Green

Lines of bright foliage, penned with care,
A laughter of leaves, in the cool, crisp air.
Each branch a story, each needle a line,
In this leafy anthology, all things intertwine.

The ferns share secrets, in a hushed tone,
While the worms write verses, in the soil they hone.
Bees buzz with humor, a trivial chat,
About fuzzy inventions, and dogs wearing hats.

With rain drops as ink, a splash and a plop,
The pages turn gently, as the raindrops drop.
Playful critters scurry, as sunlight begins,
Crafting a tale, where the laughter never ends.

So gather your thoughts, in a notebook of green,
For the flora bring stories of the great unseen.
In every nook, cranny, and bending vine,
Lives a twist of humor, and a hint of divine.

Breezes that Carry Words

A gentle breeze flutters, with whispers so light,
Tickling the leaves, in the soft twilight.
It carries each chuckle, from branch to the ground,
As giggles of critters in the forest resound.

With every soft rustle, a new tale begins,
Of ants in a picnic, and where mischief spins.
The wind is a bard, with stories to spread,
Of a turtle who danced, and an owl who read.

As daylight is fading, the whispers grow bold,
Like breezes of laughter, their warmth unfold.
With tickles from nature, shared in the glow,
The world blooms with joy, in this whimsical flow.

So listen and learn, from the breezes that play,
They'll tickle your heart, in a charming ballet.
For the words carried forth, in a twirl and a swoosh,
Bring smiles to all, in the lush and the bush.

Tranquil Thoughts Under the Canopy

Beneath the boughs, I sit so still,
A squirrel stares, my mind to fill.
It twitches its tail, a little show,
I giggle as it dances, putting on a glow.

The branches sway in whispered chats,
While I'm lost in dreams, up to their spats.
A bird sings loud, I must confess,
I can't tell if it's art or just a mess!

The sunlight pokes through leaves so bright,
Spotlight on my sandwich, a tasty sight.
But ants march in like they own the place,
I share my crumbs with such little grace.

So here I dwell, on this vibrant floor,
Where laughter rings and worries are poor.
In nature's lap, joy has no end,
Just me and my snacks, my woodland friends!

Ballad of the Forest Floor

On the forest floor, where mushrooms bloom,
Frogs strike poses like they own the room.
They leap and croak, a silly ballet,
I can't help but laugh at their grand display.

Chipmunks chatter, making a fuss,
While I trip on roots, oh what a bust!
Crawling bugs get first class views,
As I tumble down in these leafy shoes.

With each step forward, I find a surprise,
A hidden acorn, a butterfly that flies.
Nature's quirks bring a smile so wide,
Life's a comedy on this amusing ride!

So here I dance among trees so tall,
Embracing the chaos, I'm having a ball.
In this green theater, I play my part,
A jester who fills the woods with heart!

Reflections in the Pine Needles

The needles glisten like emeralds bright,
I ponder their wisdom, what's wrong or right.
Their whispers tease, like old foolish friends,
Deep thoughts emerge, but the laughter never ends.

A portrait of squirrels hangs in the air,
Each pose a joke, they don't have a care.
They slip and slide in a great little race,
While I chuckle, trying to keep pace.

Dancing shadows and sunlight rays,
Create a disco in nature's delays.
The forest floor's a gamble of fate,
With my luck, I might just be their bait!

But life's delightful in this leafy trap,
Where giggles echo as I take a nap.
Reflections sparkle, as laughter replies,
In this bouncy realm, joy never dies!

An Ode to the Tall Guardians

Oh, look at those giants, they tower so high,
With trunks so thick, they scratch at the sky.
They've seen it all, from dusk till dawn,
While I play tricks with my favorite fawn.

They whisper secrets of the winds in flight,
I imagine them gossiping day and night.
With branches swaying, they shake their heads,
As I twirl and twirl, bumping my friends' beds.

Their leaves dance down like confetti in dreams,
As I juggle acorns, bursting at the seams.
With every laugh that echoes so bold,
Their sturdy shadows keep me from cold.

So here's to the flighters, who stand straight and tall,
In this theater of magic, oh they've seen it all.
With laughter and joy, they guard merrily,
My tall, leafy friends in true harmony!

The Lullaby of Longing Pines

In the quiet woods, they sway,
Seeking buddies, come what may.
A squirrel teases, up and down,
While whispers giggle, all around.

Their needles tap like drumbeats fast,
Imagining a party, quite the blast!
But oh dear friends, they wait and pine,
For dancing feet and happy wine.

The wind sings tales of trees so tall,
Who dream of feasts, but eat no hall.
A party here, but where's the crowd?
Just leafy whispers, singing loud.

Yet still they sway, with hope so bright,
Waiting for dawn, to join the night.
For laughter's echo must descend,
Where rooted friends become pretend.

Shadows in the Forest's Embrace

In shadows thick, the branches joke,
A tree once slipped and made a poke!
The mossy ground, it giggles too,
At lumbered friends just passing through.

The owls make puns, a hoot or two,
While shadows dance, a funny crew.
They tell tall tales of bark and leaf,
And chuckle soft at their own mischief.

When dusk arrives, the hues grow bold,
The branches lean, so daring, so old.
With each gust, they shake and tease,
Turning forest lanes into a breeze.

Yet as night falls, they whisper low,
For morning brings the sun's great glow.
They sigh and yawn, with dreams in hand,
All in jest, a merry band.

Echoes of the Timbered Heart

Amidst the bark, a secret thrives,
The timbered hearts, they love their jives.
With every ring, a tale unfolds,
Of silly thoughts and bushels bold.

The forest floor is where they play,
With twigs as friends, a grand buffet.
They tease the breeze and boast their age,
As echoes dance from one to sage.

A wise old oak, with stories vast,
Shares laughs from years, both slow and fast.
While roots entwine, a friendship blessed,
With giggles whispered, they jest the best.

So if you hear a rustle near,
Don't be alarmed; just lend an ear.
For timbered hearts, in joyful plight,
Will serenade you through the night.

Songs of the Sylvan Realm

In the realm of green, the branches sway,
With rhythms that invite a playful play.
Each leaf a note on laughter's score,
As woodland creatures dance and roar.

A badger hums a catchy tune,
While rabbits hop beneath the moon.
The melody lifts, on zephyrs flown,
In a concert hall that's all their own.

The firs join in with a boisterous laugh,
Bark for percussion, a timbered staff.
Squirrels scurry, with pots and pans,
Making music in their little clans.

Yet when the sun begins to rise,
The symphony fades, but oh, what a surprise!
For dreams of tunes will surely stay,
And crawl back out for another day.

Lush Lines of Nature

In the forest where squirrels play,
A tree decided to join the fray.
It donned a hat made of leaves,
And insisted it was the grandest of thieves.

The sun peeked through with a grin,
Said, "Who knew trees had such style within?"
The bark laughed loud, its branches swayed,
With every giggle, new sap was made.

Birds chirped tunes, so offbeat and bright,
Claiming the crown for their latest flight.
While rhymes spread like pollen in the air,
The laughter of nature was always fair.

So here we gather, in this quirky glen,
Where trees tell stories again and again.
Come tune your steps to the woodland beat,
And dance with the greens, feel the rhythm of heat.

Ballads under the Pine Shade

Underneath the tall tree's crest,
A squirrel holds a tiny fest.
With acorns piled high on a plate,
It sings to friends, 'Ain't this great?'

A rabbit hops around, oh so spry,
Chiming in, 'Shall we tell a lie?'
The tree perks up, 'I'm wise, you see,
I've seen the world from A to B!'

They polished tales with twirls and spins,
And laughed so hard, the sunlight wins.
As shadows stretched long, they spun their yarns,
Creating myths of unicorns and barns.

In the end, they laughed till the moon glowed,
Every creature had cherished loads.
And thus the shade became folklore's stage,
Where nonsense flowed like a good, funny page.

Syllables among the Stumps

Amidst the stumps, a wise old owl,
Decided to host a night-time howl.
The frogs croaked in their long-winded ways,
While the owl tutored them, 'You need to amaze!'

'Hoo, hoo,' went the audience, in their best cheer,
As the crickets chirped, 'Let's bring some beer!'
The fireflies remembered how to dance,
'It's all about flair, give fun a chance!'

So syllables twinkled, jumbles in flight,
In mischief and giggles, they danced through the night.
With each passing jest, the stumps rolled round,
Becoming the throne where the laughs were found.

Come gather, all ye who crave a rhyme,
For nature's jest is the best of its time.
And as day breaks, they fade with a laugh,
But wait till twilight for encore's half!

Ode to the Woodland Whisper

In whispers soft, the trees impart,
Of all the zany things that start.
A raccoon, perched like a rockstar,
Strummed a guitar from a fallen jar.

The leaves clapped hands with a rustling sound,
As the worms wiggled up from the ground.
They formed a band, oh what a sight,
With beetles dancing under moonlight.

The mushrooms cheered, wearing caps so bright,
Swaying with glee, what a peculiar night!
Each note lifted high, like a kite in the breeze,
In the woodland's embrace, all fears would cease.

So here's to the forest, with skits so grand,
Where each tiny creature gives a helping hand.
And as dawn approaches, laughter will stay,
Echoing softly, like a gentle bouquet.

The Lament of the Larches

In a forest of tall green jesters,
Their needles tickle, they hold court,
Old Larry the Larch starts to boast,
Yet his roots give him the shortest report.

The squirrels giggle from branches above,
As he spins tales with endless spins,
"I have the biggest crown, my friends!"
But it's only a hat made of pineskin.

The winds whisper secrets, oh so sly,
As the larches grumble, full of glee,
He claims royalty, but we all know why,
His bark is worse than his roots can be.

So let's raise a toast to tall tales spun,
In this kooky wood, where laughter flows,
The larches moan, but no one's done,
Their punchlines land, where humor grows.

Harvesting the Wind's Verse.

The breezes dance, like poets in flight,
They ruffle the leaves with verses of cheer,
In this playful breeze, there's no need for fright,
As it whispers jokes for all to hear.

Oh, the gusty muse, it loves to play,
With lyrics caught in the chirp of a thrush,
A squirrel's pun ends the dullest day,
In the rustle of branches, hear the hush.

While trees chuckle at the fluttering sound,
Their limbs sway with a giggle—a chorus,
Each gust brings laughter, joy does abound,
In the orchard of whimsy, we adore us.

So let us all gather, beneath the great sky,
With the wind as our bard, we'll all be wise,
For in nature's humor, we surely can fly,
Harvesting laughter, with every reprise.

Whispers of the Evergreen

In a green world where secrets are kept,
The evergreens plot, with chuckles in mind,
Each twig holds a story, while shadows have crept,
Lighting up laughter, we're all intertwined.

A chatty old fir shares tales with a lark,
Of travelers lost and wild forest schemes,
"Why did the tree sit in the dark?"
"Because it couldn't find a branch with dreams!"

The sage in the grove throws riddles all day,
While mossy carpets laugh, rolling on ground,
Their jokes sprout like seedlings in a whimsical way,
Where silliness blooms, fun's surely found.

So listen for whispers, as branches unfold,
With giggles of saplings, life's never bland,
In this evergreen dance, laughter never grows old,
In a forest of joy, the heart is so grand.

Verses Beneath the Canopy

Under a roof of leaves, so lush and high,
The poets of nature weave verses so bright,
A coupe of owls crack puns up in the sky,
Creating a comedy, a woodland delight.

The raccoons are jesters in masks, grinning wide,
With laughter and mischief, so rich and so neat,
Their antics keep echoes, the trees take side,
As they clap their green hands, competing for beat.

Each rustling branch offers snickers and laughs,
While dappled sunbeams dance on the floor,
The wise old cedar pulls out his gaffs,
Sharing punchlines that open the door.

So come join the fun beneath leafy visual,
Where humor is plenty, and nature is free,
In the cathedral of giggles, life's ritual,
We gather in joy, just you and me.

The Rhythmic Breath of the Forest

In the woods, a squirrel twirled,
Chasing acorns as they swirled.
With a leap and a silly dance,
Who knew nuts held such romance?

The trees chuckle, their branches sway,
As shadows play hide and seek all day.
A rabbit giggles, hops with glee,
Who knew the forest was so funny?

Ink from the Heart of the Woods

A raccoon with a pen in paw,
Scratches stories that leave us in awe.
The owls hoot, in lines so tight,
While fireflies glow, creating light.

The stories swirl like leaves in the breeze,
With tales of mischief from the trees.
Whispers of joy, laughter galore,
Who knew words could be such a roar?

The Dreamer's Grove

In a grove where shadows stretch wide,
Dreamers gather with hearts open wide.
They toss their wishes to the sky,
And giggles echo as they pass by.

A bubble floats with a wish inside,
Finding a buddy, they take a ride.
With each pop, a chuckle erupts,
In this grove, laughter disrupts.

Words Carried in the Wind

The wind carries tales from afar,
Whispered secrets, like a twinkling star.
The breeze tickles the leaves on high,
As giggles scatter, soaring by.

With every gust, a joke takes flight,
Telling the trees to hold on tight.
They sway and bob, laughing out loud,
In a symphony, nature's proud.

Lyrical Echoes in the Glade

In the glade where branches sway,
A squirrel sings to start the day.
He lost a nut, it's quite the mess,
But hey, it's nature's morning dress.

Leaves giggle as the breezes tease,
Twirling round the ancient trees.
A chipmunk laughs, what a sight,
Dancing shadows, pure delight.

The sunlight winks through leafy seams,
Creating patches for our dreams.
With roots entwined, they scheme and play,
Making mirth in their own way.

So gather round, my friends, and see
The woodland's charm and wild glee.
In every nook, a jest awaits,
In nature's arms, we celebrate!

The Abyss of Green Shadows

In a realm where shadows stretch wide,
A lizard thinks he's got a ride.
On a snail's back, what a bold move!
But off they go, not quite in groove.

The owls hoot with a cheeky grin,
While crickets strike up their din.
A bear sneezes, starts a quake,
And all the trees begin to shake!

The shadows twirl, a dance of tricks,
While bees get caught in a sticky mix.
A whisper here, a giggle there,
Life unfurls without a care!

So join the frolic, feel the cheer,
In green abyss, let's draw near.
For laughs abound beneath the sky,
In nature's playground, oh my, oh my!

Musings in the Shade

Underneath the leafy boughs,
A wise old tortoise makes his vows.
To never rush, take every road,
While ants parade, a tiny load.

With twigs as swords, the kids convene,
As dragonflies make quite the scene.
"Catch me if you can!" they shout,
The tree trunks chuckle, no doubt!

The shadows weave a playful mirth,
While rabbits scheme for their next hearth.
In every rustle, giggles rise,
As nature plays its funny guise.

So settle back, enjoy the shade,
In this wild world, fun's not delayed.
With every breeze, a punchline spins,
In leafy realms where laughter begins!

Timeless Touch of the Trees

With a patter of feet on mossy ground,
A wise old tree speaks without sound.
"Life's a jest, just look around!"
In whispers soft, the leaves are wound.

The branches sway with a comical grace,
While squirrels race in a nutty chase.
A beetle struts, dressed to the nines,
Claiming spots like a star that shines!

The roots below, they shimmy and sway,
As shadows flirt and come out to play.
With every rustle, a laugh takes flight,
In nature's glow, everything's bright.

So let's embrace this earthy cheer,
With every giggle in the atmosphere.
In timeless woods where joy resounds,
Life's lighthearted dance forever abounds!

Enchantment by the Evergreen

In a forest strange, where whispers play,
The trees wear coats of green today.
Squirrels prance in a quirky dance,
While birds debate their latest romance.

A pine cone drops, oh what a sight,
Rolling down with reckless delight.
The sunbeams giggle, tickling leaves,
As nature spins her tale of reprieves.

Branches chuckle, their stories entwined,
In a world where laughter is always signed.
Moss carpets soft, the ground it's dressed,
Among the roots, the fairies rest.

So here we stand, in this playful grove,
Where every tree has secrets to strove.
Nature's jesters, in earthy attire,
Invite us all to join the choir.

Soliloquy of the Forest Floor

Beneath the canopy, shrouded in shade,
A carpet of needles, a leafy parade.
Worms tell tales that wiggle and squirm,
As mushrooms pop with a cheeky charm.

Ants march boldly, a conga line,
Each tiny critter, a friend of divine.
Grumpy old toads sit with a frown,
While the chatty crickets dance around town.

The breeze carries giggles through every tree,
Perhaps the woodland spirits join in for free.
With every rustle, a chorus is born,
In this merry realm of the understated and worn.

So listen closely to the ground's funny fate,
Where even a pebble can debate and create.
In this wild dance, both silly and sweet,
The forest floor hosts a whimsical beat.

Melodies of the Majestic Bough

Up in the branches, the songs take flight,
The breezes hum tunes under moonlight.
Nightingales croon in a chorus sublime,
While owls rehearse their wisecracking rhyme.

A squirrel sidesteps, a performer at heart,
Stealing the show, he's a true work of art.
His acorn stash, a prize to defend,
With antics and tricks that never quite end.

Under stars, the woodpecker knocks,
While raccoons plot in their kingly frocks.
The trees sway gently, grooving their roots,
As nature's minstrels display their flutes.

Oh sing, dear branches, the tales you've amassed,
In this merry woodland, where laughter is cast.
The canopy laughs at the antics below,
As magic and mischief continually grow.

Shadows and Scribbles

In the twilight's glow, a sketchbook lays,
With doodles of critters in whimsical ways.
A fox in a top hat, oh what a sight,
Dipping a paw in the ink just right.

The shadows waltz, they jiggle and sway,
As squirrels pop out for a late-night play.
Each stroke of the brush reveals a new grin,
In this gallery where the fun begins.

Crickets compose the orchestra's sound,
As the little night creatures all gather 'round.
With whispers of magic that swirl in the air,
The echoes of laughter, a melody rare.

So scribble and splash, let the wild pens flow,
In this playful place, let creativity grow.
From shadows to scribbles, the night soars high,
With a dose of humor beneath the starry sky.

www.ingramcontent.com/pod-product-compliance
Lightning Source LLC
Chambersburg PA
CBHW071829160426
43209CB00003B/245